# IMPRESSIONS

RASHMI MENON

Copyright © Rashmi Menon
All Rights Reserved.

*I would like to dedicate this book to "My little bundle of joy " my daughter who makes me reflect on the untold joys of Life and form better impressions about the world around me.*

# Contents

# Contents

# Preface

*"Take, if you must, this little bag of dreams, unloose the cord, and they will wrap you around.*

*William Butler Yeats*

*This is what my book **"Impressions** "(A short Collection of poems) is all about. It is an attempt from an amateur poetic soul to bring my little bag of dreams and unloose the cord, through the canvass of my words the pictures etched in my mind that have left lasting impressions on me.*

*It attempts to bring out the importance of our thoughts and emotions in our daily lives. How they leave an indelible imprint on each one of us. We form impressions of almost every experience in life and to bring out those memories and emotions is an attempt of mine.*

*I hope somewhere it leaves a deep impression on your minds and resonates with experiences from our daily lives*

# Acknowledgements

*I thank all of you with whom I have directly or indirectly interacted and who have left their footprints on my life. Thank you to the invincible power that has looked after me from the moment I was born.*

*I would like to thank my parents and my brother for giving me the motivation to pursue my dreams and follow my heart and for their unconditional support through every phase of my life. My husband and daughter for giving me the inspiration and support to come out with this collection of poems.*

*To my teachers, friends, colleagues, and family gratitude is all I have for their presence in my life, for shaping my thoughts and guiding me as I move forward.*

*And to my publisher ''Poetic souls "to bring my little bag of dreams to the pages of a book.*

# About The Author

*From god's own country, I am an army officer's daughter and have been lucky enough to travel through diverse Indian states. Interacting with diverse communities, people of different faiths, and cultures. My schooling has been in Convents as well as Kendriya Vidyalaya. I completed my degree in Applied Psychology and have a degree in Masters of Business administration. I have around 12 years of work experience in varied fields, Banking, Call center, Recruitment, Counselling, and Teaching. My work experiences coloured my perceptions and helped me evolve as a better person and made me more human. It has contributed today to creating my book on "Impressions."*

*Today I am a mother to a beautiful five-year-old daughter bubbling with energy and my husband has been my constant pillar of support in all my life decisions. Lucky and blessed enough to be supported by my extended family of in-laws, aunts, uncles, cousins, friends, and colleagues the list goes on in all my endeavors!*

# CHAPTER ONE

# Rainbow Calling

*In love and happy is the Bridal Red,*
*With sacred thread and soul walks the Orange Monk,*
*Seasons change with yellow Daffodils,*
*For all, we know in the garden of Eden was a green, green*
*serpent,*
*A painter's heaven is the divine Blue,*
*Freedom by peasants started with Indigo,*
*In violet, we find the new-age love,*
*The spectrum of life in its myriad hues,*
*It's the rainbow calling after all.*

*Red, Green, and Blue make the divine White,*
*The Sunsets and Sunrises are all scarlet Red,*
*The Cardinal Red makes way for courage and sacrifice,*
*The Crimson lake was the painter's delight,*
*The Starry night with orange stars could never have been*
*imagined,*
*The Canary bird sings the lullaby as sweet as can be,*
*With the Orange revolutions, history changed its course,*
*The imperial Yellow or mellow Yellow choose what you*
*may,*
*For the Lord, himself believes in the symphony,*
*The Mona Lisa in green couldn't have looked nobler,*

*Muhammed in hadith said "water, greenery, and a
beautiful face" were good things,
In virgin Mary, we discovered the blue,
Royal blue was the colour of the kings and now the
commoner wears denim blue,
Newton may have seen the seventh indigo, just like the
seven notes and the seven planets,
The colour of vanity is violet, "Viola"! meant good
memories, loving thoughts, and souvenirs,
And lavender fields show beauty with peace and grace for
a higher purpose,
The spectrum of life in its myriad hues,
It's the rainbow calling after all.*

# CHAPTER TWO

# The colour of my skin

*Does it matter so much I ask?*
*I may be born brown, white, or black forever,*
*I maybe not be so evil or unlucky,*
*Fair is not the world,*
*Fair is not the colour of my skin,*
*Hidden behind this dark truth was just like you a loving,*
*beautiful soul,*
*Ugly was what they said, never to be accepted,*
*Prejudiced by the colour of my skin, life was never the*
*same,*
*Looking for a job or a partner I thought maybe,*
*If I could paint myself white, so that I may be more divine,*
*It caused me so much hurt and pain for the world to see*
*only my skin.*
*Does it matter so much I ask?*
*For black was not what I chose, but what god blessed me*
*with,*
*In history, we survived despite the tone of our skin,*
*We have been around for more than a billion years,*
*Africa, America, Britain, Australia, Brazil we are*
*everywhere,*
*So, I understand now, that fair is not the only world there*
*exists,*

*They wear black to mourn the loss of their friend,*
*Now I realize it was to mourn the loss of their dead soul,*
*For me, the colour black brings alchemy of life and death.*

# CHAPTER THREE

# What if....?

*What if there were no sunsets?*
*What if there were no moonlit nights?*
*What if the sea was silent?*
*What if the flowers won't blossom?*
*What if the bees won't buzz?*
*What if it doesn't rain or snow?*
*What if birds don't chirp?*
*Never does the sun or the moon know,*
*Never does the sea know,*
*Never does the bee or flower know,*
*Never does the rain or snow know,*
*The sounds of silence that surround us,*
*Is it just an illusion?*
*Or another day in paradise?*

# CHAPTER FOUR

# Invincible soul

*When no one could hear me cry,*
*When no one could see me,*
*When no one could hug me,*
*When I could not hold on to anyone,*
*I felt I was heard and seen,*
*Those tears rolled and stopped,*
*I knew I was being watched,*
*I knew I being loved,*
*I knew I was being cared for,*
*Nothing else mattered as I walked down this long arduous*
*road,*
*For I was not alone there was an invincible soul in*
*disguise,*
*For every breath I took,*
*For every thought I had,*
*For every joy I experienced,*
*For every sadness, I felt,*
*I was forever grateful to this Invincible soul,*
*I may not have been perfect but he showed me a path that*
*would give me unending joy.*

# CHAPTER FIVE

# Early In Life

*Is it the most difficult thing to see your child fall?*
*Have they healed alright?*
*Will they come out fine?*
*Then I remember the days when I was young,*
*For every fall of mine, when I got up on my own,*
*I learned to heal from deep inside,*
*That's what sets us free in this life,*
*For them to fight their battles better in life,*
*We must learn to let go of them early in life,*
*What's holding us inside is the fear that harm may come,*
*and shield them every time,*
*But we need to know the needs of the times,*
*Let them fall without you behind,*
*For every time they fail, you have won the fight,*
*It's their world let them decide early in life,*
*And learn what it takes to grow and survive,*
*For ruthless will be the world when you are not around*
*and they need to come out stronger,*
*To grow up takes courage and not just might,*
*Let them grow as they fall in front of your eyes.*

# CHAPTER SIX

# Dreams

*This is my world of dreams,*
*A little different from the world where we think,*
*Some days I can touch the blue, blue sky and fly to the*
*moon and back,*
*This kaleidoscope of dreams has everything you can only*
*imagine,*
*A world where people think without fear,*
*Free from shackles of age and gender,*
*Where colour, race, and wealth don't matter,*
*A world free from misery, pain, and hurt,*
*Where life is precious for every moment you lived,*
*Where nature heals all your wounds,*
*Where we can open our hearts and can be heard,*
*Where we don't feel lonely and sad,*
*In this dream, I hear heartbeats skip for every moment we*
*live,*
*The sound of music from all things alive,*
*Far away is the land of my dreams for when I wake up*
*The blue, blue sky smiles at me, this is just a dream of*
*mine!*

# CHAPTER SEVEN

# Grandma's Coin

*On a rainy day when grandma gave me a coin,*
*I didn't know what was it for, so I asked?*
*She said piggy knows so put the coin,*
*Piggy saved my dream for me,*
*and I got my favourite toy on my birthday,*
*as I grew older piggy became my best friend,*
*Little did I know on a rainy day he would be there to*
*comfort me,*
*Little did I know what grandma meant on that rainy day*
*Saving the coin was the most precious lesson of my life,*
*Many years later I understood what saving for a rainy day*
*meant!*

# Be a child

*When I saw them roll in the mud,*
*All they were saying was "Do the things you love to do "*
*When I heard them say "I shared my toys today "*
*All they were saying was "Share your joys every day "*
*When I heard them laugh their hearts out,*
*All they were saying was "Smile for no reason "*
*When I heard their cry,*
*All they were saying was "it's okay to cry when in pain "*
*When I heard them say "I love you, mommy"*
*All they were saying simply was "You are precious to me "*
*When I saw her paint on the wall*
*All they were saying was "Use your imagination "*
*When I saw her play run and talk all day long,*
*All they were saying was "I have a carefree life "*
*Being a child sometimes was the only way to look at life!*

# CHAPTER NINE

# In War and Peace

*In War and Peace,*
*We are told of tales that cannot be told,*
*We see a double-edged sword being used by countries*
*galore,*
*In whom do we believe for death hangs by a thin thread,*
*Does fear tap on the Soldier's shoulder at war?*
*For brave are those who were never Soldiers,*
*but fought the battles with a conflicted mind,*
*In War and Peace,*
*I may die a thousand deaths by not saving my countrymen*
*said the leader once,*
*So we fought a war to save our nation,*
*And made peace with my enemies when the time was*
*right,*
*Till then let there be bloodshed on the streets, for we are*
*fighting for what is ours,*
*Is the land with only death beds the future we want to see?*
*Marred wounds are left for time to heal,*
*Alas! In war and peace, you only see the Lost world and*
*lost Souls,*
*In War and peace what should prevail is hope for better*
*mankind.*

# CHAPTER TEN

# Memories of my Grandmother

*Clinging on to her sari as a child, those were happy days,*
*The smell of her special cooking and savouries is all that*
*we could dream of,*
*We jumped with joy every time we managed to hide and*
*she would come and seek us out,*
*The Chandan on her forehead and bangle on her bare*
*hands and a watch to tell her ahead of time,*
*Listening and sleeping and hearing her lullabies there was*
*nothing more peaceful than that,*
*Then came those humorous stories where lord Krishna*
*would ride an autorickshaw to heaven!*
*The laughter we had and giggles bonded us as cousins for*
*a lifetime,*
*As we grew up we saw the wrinkles on her face, but still*
*felt like clinging to her sari,*
*Only now she clung onto me, for all that she gave me she*
*wanted it all back,*
*Life had come a full circle for I saw the child in her,*
*As I lost her in front of me I wish I could have told her my*
*little secret prayer,*

RASHMI MENON

*I wanted her to see my daughter before she left for her
abode and lucky, I was,
The little angel bought all my granny wished for laughter
and unbridled joy.*

# CHAPTER ELEVEN

# Womb

*I am a girl and I don't want to carry the child in my womb,*
*Life has just begun for me how can I give life to another?*
*I am a woman and I am not sure if I want to carry the*
*child in my womb,*
*Can life give me another chance?*
*I am a mother and don't want to carry another child in my*
*womb for I am human,*
*Maybe I cannot look after them!*
*I have been raped and where are the humans who want me*
*to be human?*
*How can I even carry the child in my womb?*
*Is it for me to decide or for others who don't live my life,*
*What we have lost is not our life but our souls,*
*So when do I want to carry the child?*
*Is that what you want to know?*
*It's when love and respect for me as a woman exist, for I*
*am as human as you.*

# CHAPTER TWELVE

# Rituals our Saviour

*For generations to come there was always a ritual,*
*We always did the rituals without asking why,*
*Would it help us in overcoming the struggles of our daily*
*life?*
*These sacred sacraments were to go beyond this world at*
*the end,*
*For improving our lives and removing undesirable*
*attributes,*
*So the rituals came before conception to cremation,*
*For the unborn child and a male heir!*
*For the mother's womb and healthy child,*
*For naming a child and learning the alphabet,*
*The sacred thread initiation to the end of education,*
*From Marriage to death a ritual for every phase,*
*These rituals that we followed were never blindly written,*
*For us to understand it may take some time,*
*For generations to come there will always be a ritual,*
*Rituals may be our saviour inadvertently for a better life.*

# CHAPTER THIRTEEN

# Shackles

*I grew up liking all colours,*
*but I was told pink is only for you,*
*I grew up wearing shorts,*
*but I was told skirts are for you,*
*I grew up having short hair,*
*I was told long hair was meant for you,*
*I grew up playing with cars,*
*I was told dolls are meant for you,*
*because I was a girl life was never the same,*
*Time went by and now I am a woman,*
*I was still told about things to do!*
*I did not get married to the lucky guy,*
*but I was told marriage is a must for you,*
*I did not have a child of my own,*
*but I was told that's why I was born,*
*So I broke all these shackles and became what I wanted to*
*be*
*For life is short and all the shackles were not meant for*
*me!*

# CHAPTER FOURTEEN

# Love is bittersweet

*Love is what fools do,*
*So, I was young and foolish*
*I fell in love under the moonlit sky,*
*I fell in love with the roses,*
*I fell in love with those eyes,*
*I fell in love with that smile,*
*I fell in love with the voice,*
*Love is what fools do and we broke up one fine day*
*Then I got married on an auspicious day,*
*I fell in love again under the moonlit sky,*
*I fell in love with the roses,*
*I fell in love with those eyes,*
*I fell in love with his smile,*
*I fell in love with how he thought for I was not foolish and*
*young anymore,*
*But then we parted ways after some time,*
*Perhaps it was love that eluded me,*
*I may not be a fool after all because love is bittersweet.*

# CHAPTER FIFTEEN

# " I am not queer "

*For years together I may have been ostracized,*
*I am not queer but just like you I lead a normal life,*
*For you may wonder what is this life?*
*I may have been shunned from celebrations of life,*
*Rebuked for the way I feel and look and what I like,*
*For years together I have been around,*
*So, what if I was born a girl and feel like a man,*
*In life, many of us feel trapped for it takes courage to take*
*wings and fly,*
*Living this life is a fight for survival but as long as you*
*accept me for who I am,*
*I will live my dreams and hope for a bright future,*
*Love me for no other reason but just like you I am another*
*human*

# CHAPTER SIXTEEN

# Unending Wait

*I am sitting on the porch of my new home,*
*Waiting eagerly for a visit by a loved one,*
*As time goes by, I am only surrounded by memories,*
*Pictures of those happy days and times passed by,*
*As I look back and wonder what happened in all those*
*years?*
*I looked after my children, did everything for them,*
*Today I am lonely because I cared for them?*
*I may be old and my vision poor, I may not be able to walk*
*that fast,*
*But my thoughts run fast to the days I spend talking with*
*my kids,*
*Teaching them to look after themselves,*
*A stranger has been kind, visits me often, and just listens*
*me out,*
*For I wonder life is stranger than I thought for I find*
*solace not in my child anymore,*
*I may be old and wise but life has never been so unkind,*
*for I have no answers only stories to tell,*
*I miss my soulmate but life as they say goes on, this wait is*
*unending, not my life,*
*I am sitting on the porch of my new home,*
*Waiting eagerly for a visit by a loved one.*

# CHAPTER SEVENTEEN

# A verdict of heaven or hell ?

*Who is to say if the verdict will be heaven or hell?*
*For the path, we have chosen on this earth,*
*They say you get roses in heaven,*
*And thorns in hell,*
*One cannot do without the other, choose what you want,*
*The path that you choose has to be with care,*
*For even the roses may wither in heaven,*
*And thorns may not prick in hell,*
*You may choose to sin or do good as they say,*
*Who is to say if the verdict will be heaven or hell?*
*For if both the doors close and are forbidden for us,*
*Does it matter what verdict we get heaven or hell?*
*The verdict is out here, on earth you will experience both*
*your heaven and hell!*
*And try as you may you cannot escape this verdict of life.*

# CHAPTER EIGHTEEN

# Someone who I used to know

*Sometime back I met a stranger, then we came to know each
other,*
*Somewhere later we parted ways, only to meet each other
again,*
*For someone that I used to know, there was a change that
I could not embrace,*
*As I spend some time I came to know it's important to let
go of those memories,*
*For someone that I used to know may have forgotten those
days long ago,*
*Life has transformed and bought changes galore,*
*Once it was the small things that gave us joy,*
*Now the big things deluded our joy,*
*There is little hope in the coming days that we are
together,*
*For someone that I used to know,*
*Time has left its indelible mark.*

# CHAPTER NINETEEN

# Recipes of emotions

*A pinch of sadness and I was fortunate in love,*
*A pinch of jealousy that amused me no end,*
*A pinch of guilt that made me shameless to no end,*
*A pinch of grief that made me miss someone,*
*A pinch of anger then peace prevailed,*
*A pinch of calmness that eased out the tension,*
*A pinch of adoration that made us smile,*
*A pinch of boredom for the next inspiration,*
*A pinch of fear for the courage to appear,*
*A pinch of romance on a rainy day,*
*A pinch of excitement for something new,*
*A pinch of awkwardness for that made me true,*
*A pinch of nostalgia for those days,*
*And here I was with recipes of emotions!*

# CHAPTER TWENTY

# Dreams Disintegrated

*When I was young and famous my dreams disintegrated,*
*What I thought was good disillusioned me to no end,*
*But what were those dreams that were fragmented?*
*Those were dreams about a life together with people I*
*loved,*
*But things changed with fame and wealth,*
*Life was never the same with no time for my loved ones,*
*And what mattered was how I looked and what I wore,*
*Gone were the days when I was accepted for what I did,*
*Now I pay the price and my dreams are disintegrated,*
*This was the world I lived for, everything I dreamt of,*
*Then came the answer do what you do and integrate your*
*dreams,*
*Live for yourself and not the fame that you seek,*
*And that's how I saved my life and dreams from*
*disintegrating.*

# CHAPTER TWENTY-ONE

# Habits tucked away

*Like a cup of coffee with the sunrise every day,*
*That gave me light on a gloomy day,*
*These were habits of mine tucked away for years together I*
*say,*
*Like a cup of piping hot tea on a cold winter morning,*
*Which cleared the thick fog on my mind every day,*
*These were habits of mine tucked away for years together I*
*say,*
*Like a walk with an umbrella on a rainy day,*
*that saved me from a lot of trouble,*
*These were habits of mine tucked away for years together I*
*say,*
*Like the box of letters that I treasured every day,*
*These habits brought me closer to the loved ones far away,*
*It was my habit tucked away for years together I say,*
*Like the box of chocolates that would melt when I ate it*
*every day,*
*It melted my heart for love this sweet was a treat,*
*These habits of mine tucked away in time were the only*
*ways I knew how to live this life every day.*

# CHAPTER TWENTY-TWO

# Speaking mirror

*Only if the mirror could speak,*
*For I wished to know if I was as beautiful as before,*
*Life has never been the same, for my face has been marred*
*by burns,*
*For everyone told me it was not the end, how could I*
*believe this life of lies,*
*My mind was encumbered with thoughts, does love deserve*
*this fate I thought?*
*I did not want this pity for myself, for I would see myself in*
*the mirror every day,*
*Just when life seems unforgiving, the mirror spoke to me,*
*Look deep inside of you and you will heal,*
*And as time went by the wounds had healed,*
*And then love knocked on the door,*
*This time it was me who was in love with myself,*
*And looked more beautiful than ever before,*
*I guess the mirror did show me a different side.*

# CHAPTER TWENTY-THREE

# Life with Dignity

*The only light that I could see, was the earthen lamp lit
outside my house,
For days and years had gone by and there was no respite,
Lying on the bed there was only anguish and eyes that
could only see darkness,
For even the tears in my eyes had dried up and there was
no light at the end of the tunnel,
And then came a moment where I saw the light and was
weary no more,
For who is to say if this was mercy for me or my loved
ones,
But this was what I wanted the only hope for my incurable
pain,
Have mercy on my life and set me free!
For I wanted to live this life with dignity and no more
agonize in pain.*

# CHAPTER TWENTY-FOUR

# Modern Times

*A cup of coffee, food gobbled down and I am off to work,*
*I took a taxi to my work, sometimes it was the metro that*
*saved my day,*
*And then there was the onerous boss, who was looking*
*forward to make my day,*
*Pushing me to meet a deadline, I am glad I was alive at the*
*end of the day,*
*The endless wait and traffic, insured heading back home*
*was nothing short of a delight,*
*These were modern times.*
*Then jaded one day, I asked myself is this what I want*
*from life?*
*So, I gave up the comforts of this modern life,*
*Moved away from the city that gave me no joy,*
*It was the sound of chirping birds that woke me up now*
*every day,*
*No more caught in the rush of life I had a piece of land to*
*survive,*
*The lush green fields in times to come were the dreams*
*that I had now,*
*No choking on smoking air, there was abundant fresh air,*
*I had now time for everyone I cared about, life had*
*transformed and I was jaded no more,*

*These were the changes that I made, for these were modern times.*

# CHAPTER TWENTY-FIVE

# Make a room for me

*Here I come make room for me,*
*They know me as "sadness ",*
*I know you may not want me,*
*For fleeting happiness could not wait for me,*
*For days you may not have missed me at all,*
*I may take your empty space so hold on to it till you can,*
*Here I come make room for me.*

*Knowing me may seem familiar,*
*And I may have left you last with truncated affection for*
*me,*
*For if you understand me well then,*
*You may not ever want to leave me alone,*
*You may have made room for many but not me,*
*So now when you make room for me you might get the key*
*to everlasting happiness!*

# CHAPTER TWENTY-SIX

# Life is freaking insane

*For who is to say I am sane?*
*Strange is the world that leaves me alone when I am*
*insane,*
*There is no single man sane I say,*
*When you see innocent people dying in war,*
*When you see innocent children injured or abandoned,*
*For when you can't walk as you used to and there is only*
*pity for you,*
*When women are treated as if they are non-existent,*
*When you are an outcast for not being from the same*
*caste,*
*For when you are judged only for your appearance,*
*For when you are not young anymore and old age seems a*
*burden,*
*For when I shamed for things I might have not done,*
*For letting down that heavy bundle of expectations set on*
*me,*
*For when I was charged guilty for a crime I did not*
*commit,*
*There is only one truth to cover these hundred lies,*
*That life is not freaking sane, or eccentric, am I?*

# CHAPTER TWENTY-SEVEN

# Whom do I Idolize

*Every waking moment I asked who did I idolise?*
*Who has changed the way I looked at life,*
*When I stopped in my path not knowing where to go,*
*Who showed me the way ahead where uncertainty was all*
*over me,*
*In my deepest darkest moments who showed me the light,*
*I realized they were not someone far away,*
*Mostly they were ordinary people whom I met on the*
*streets,*
*When I saw the salesman making his sales pitch on a grim*
*day,*
*When I saw the vendor selling tea on a cold winter*
*morning,*
*When I saw the old man teaching children on the street for*
*free,*
*When I saw an old lady running every single day in the*
*morning,*
*When I saw kids going to school every single day,*
*When I saw the doctor treating a patient risking his own*
*life,*
*You learned about not giving up on your dreams,*
*You learned money was not the only thing that mattered,*
*You learned that age was just a number,*

*The value of education in our lives for a better future,*
*How resilient we were in our daily lives,*
*There are many idols whom I idolized,*
*But ordinary people whom I met on the streets left many*
*impressions on me.*
*These were perhaps the people whom I idolized*
*unknowingly!*

# Fortitude

*The fear of failure drove me to perfection,*
*The fear of being judged, I found my true worth,*
*The fear of intimacy may have made me cold,*
*The fear of success made me think hard about my dreams,*
*The fear of unknowns and I became more comfortable*
*with knowns,*
*The fear of rejection many a time may have left me timid*
*and intimidated,*
*The fear of my loss may have kept me close to my loved*
*ones,*
*Each time the fears were different,*
*And I still may not have embraced all of them,*
*For it took courage to build this fortitude,*
*For if I were infallible then maybe I am not me anymore!*

# Unspoken feelings

I hated you when you gave away our secret,
I was angry because you betrayed me,
I was jealous to see you in love,
I felt guilty about hiding the truth,
I was sad to lose my loved one,
I was happy to see you full of smiles,
I was thankful that I had a roof over my head,
I wanted to say sorry for the hurt I caused,
I was hoping you would forgive me for my actions,
I was disappointed with what he did for me,
I lost faith by virtue of his actions,
Many moments in our lives glide away,
Sometimes fear, sometimes inhibitions,
Stopped me from giving voice to these unspoken feelings
of mine.

# CHAPTER THIRTY

# Do I See ?

*Do I see the snowfall?*
*The white snow and winter chills,*
*Do I see the rainfall?*
*A cloudy day and muddy footprints,*
*Do I see the shining sun?*
*The scorching heat and sweating souls,*
*Do I see the autumn leaves?*
*In all its shades,*
*Do I see the young woman smile?*
*The light in her eyes,*
*Do I see the man in love?*
*Who cannot think clearly anymore,*
*Do I see the tears of joy?*
*As they hold their baby for the first time,*
*Do I see the small child in the old woman?*
*Craving for ice cream,*
*Even if don't,*
*I know I am not alone,*
*I am not the only one blind,*
*Sometimes you miss these moments even with open eyes!*

# CHAPTER THIRTY-ONE

# Strangers we met on the train

*Every time we travelled on the train,*
*We had fellow travellers who were strangers on our*
*journey on the train,*
*As time went by, we shared our meals and had some small*
*talk,*
*Sometimes it was the food that broke the ice and*
*sometimes the children shook hands,*
*Sometimes it was the uncomfortable exchanging of seats*
*or making space for excess baggage.*

*For this was the journey that I missed as time went by,*
*It may be a long journey but this made it worthwhile,*
*Perfect strangers would open up about their lives,*
*There were no pretensions, even if we had to part ways at*
*the next station,*
*There was no rush for we had time to kill and laughed*
*heartily,*
*As the journey came to an end, we bid adieu and wished*
*each other well,*
*For they were strangers we met on the train who*
*sometimes became lifelong friends.*

# CHAPTER THIRTY-TWO

# Mistakes

*Every time I made a mistake, I feared the repercussions,*
*More than that felt awful about misconstruing the situation,*
*And felt dreadful that I had misread people's intentions,*
*For I may have caused hurt knowingly or unknowingly,*
*How could I undo this hurt, was it as simple as apologizing?*

*Every time I made a mistake, I feared the repercussions,*
*The person wronged may decide to be unforgiving,*
*As I grew older I knew it was not something one can control,*
*I only hoped we could forget and forgive, was it so hard?*
*These were the most formidable consequences in life,*
*Did I regret all the mistakes that I made?*
*Some made me wiser, some made me regret,*
*For life is unforgiving at times for mistakes we make,*
*But these mistakes made me who I am today perhaps more*
*human.*

# CHAPTER THIRTY-THREE

# Comedy of Complex Society

*Child marriage was celebrated with gaiety,*
*A widow remarried was disdained upon,*
*It was Child's play for someone who could destroy a child's*
*life,*
*And was revered as a saint among many,*
*For this was the comedy of the complex society.*

*I was not from another space, I was a man from this race,*
*But was discriminated against based on my colour, caste,*
*and race,*
*Every time I was in this mad race, I lost out to the evils of*
*our race*
*For this was the comedy of our complex society.*

*I was born a man, I could not cry like a woman, for I may*
*be scorned upon,*
*But if I laughed at everything gay, I was a man of this*
*world,*
*Then if I was a man with power and got away with*
*everything inane,*

*It may be inglorious to say but this was the comedy of this complex society.*

# CHAPTER THIRTY-FOUR

# Pandemic times

*The silence was killing me for I was used to noise,*
*There was fear that grappled everyone the same,*
*It was fear of the unknown,*
*and I consoled myself by saying that my loved ones were near,*
*For days passed by and we sat together for meals,*
*There was gratitude for every moment we had together,*
*Life was always uncertain that became certain,*
*So, we lived it second by second, and in the moment,*
*Then came one day when it came knocking at our door,*
*And we faced our fears, the only way out,*
*The worst may not have been over but blessed were those who were alive,*
*And that we were in it together,*
*Some strangers helped each other for no other reason but that they were humans,*
*That made a difference and we were now stronger than ever,*
*Who was to say what was the future,*
*Time went by and we lived through these pandemic times,*
*Only to value more what was once taken for granted "Our precious life "*

# CHAPTER THIRTY-FIVE

# "My Little Bundle of Joy "

*The dream I had long ago came true one fine day,*
*So here I was years later with "My little bundle of joy ",*
*Tears trickled down my eyes and they would not stop,*
*For I discovered what unconditional love was all about,*
*It felt like she was part of me much before she was born,*
*Her eyes shined so bright that would make the moon shy*
*away,*
*Her smile was a godsend gift for it lit up my otherwise*
*weary world,*
*She looked at me with her eager eyes and my life was*
*about to change forever.*


*For they said you may not feel the same since you did not go*
*through pain,*
*Who is to know the truth but we shared the same agony of*
*not having a child,*
*And then life changed the moment I held those tiny hands,*
*You knew what was being told was not true,*
*I may not be as ready as others for the lies ahead but that's*
*what I chose to take,*

*What was certain was it was going to be an incredible journey ahead,*
*She came from my heart that was full of love for this was*
*"My little bundle of joy "*

# CHAPTER THIRTY-SIX

# Change and Time

*The struggle for our freedom was long to free ourselves from*
*subservience,*
*Then at the stroke of midnight, it was time for a change,*
*We freed our country from the ruthless plundering that has*
*still left a mark,*
*For this was a long journey that change and time took*
*together.*

*It took years together to have this new age wonder,*
*There are many untold stories to be told for generations to*
*come,*
*For each man, his worth build this nation from brick to brick,*
*For this was a long journey that change and time took*
*together.*

*There are now women fighting on the battlefield,*
*And drones help farmers look after their fields,*
*We have discovered new life and looked beyond the moon,*
*For this was a long journey that change and time took*
*together.*

*We had once the leisure of looking at change and time*
*together,*
*Now we don't even sit together for values have changed,*
*It was now time to look back and wonder what has changed?*
*We need to look harder and ask did we change for the better?*
*There are now more than a billion walking together on this*
*road*
*So are changes and times drifting apart?*

# CHAPTER THIRTY-SEVEN

# Blue Envelopes

*Once they were part of our lives now no more,*
*Letters that pulled the strings of my heart all the time,*
*They were from loved ones far apart written with a lot of*
*thought,*
*Some from my friends, some from my uncles, some from*
*my cousins,*
*They bought me closer even though we were miles apart,*
*I could imagine their world and they could see mine*
*through those words.*
*Those blue envelopes may have been long forgotten,*
*But I treasure them more than my gold bangles,*
*For they comfort my soul even today as no one could,*
*They were written long back from memories etched in the*
*mind,*
*Cherished for a long they were my long-lost friends,*
*Handwritten in ink those were notes that I treasure the*
*most,*
*Every time I saw the letterbox full of those blue envelopes,*
*I would jump with joy and lose my blues for a very long*
*time!*

# CHAPTER THIRTY-EIGHT

# I never understood what was it to be a man !

*I never understood what was it to be a man,*
*for I was born a woman in this life,*
*He may have flexed his muscles for a fight as a man,*
*While I may have looked into the mirror a thousand times,*
*I would cry at the drop of a hat and he would only show*
*those tears behind,*
*He would be worried about the petrol in the car,*
*While I would be humming to the radio sound,*
*Sometimes time would have clocked faster in his life and*
*aged him faster than I,*
*For I did not understand the stress in his life for I thought I*
*shared some of his burdens now.*


*I never understood what was it for a man,*
*For I was born a woman in this life,*
*I only knew of expectations and how to judge a man,*
*Even if I had not lived their life,*

*I may have carried for nine months a child but for him,*
*It was an unending wait for what would change his life,*
*He may not have been taught to articulate his heart,*
*He only spoke of what was on his mind,*
*For he has taken care of all significant others in his life*
*and that's what weighed his mind,*
*As time passed, we understood each other better,*
*and I saw him as a man who looked after his woman just*
*fine.*

# CHAPTER THIRTY-NINE

# The Seven Vows

*Till death do us part we took those seven vows,*
*We got married one fine day many years back,*
*Times may have changed but not the promises we made,*
*When we look back today it's the vows that made us stay,*
*For we wished each other good health and a life full of joy,*
*To give courage and strength to each other through all times,*
*And that we were in it together with our families not far behind,*
*Even if stayed miles apart, the vows that we made tied us together,*
*For we may have had many differences, but life bought us closer,*
*We could have drifted apart but we kept our faith during difficult times,*
*Times may have changed and we may have become rusted and old,*
*And may have also forgotten those vows but now all that matters,*
*That we wish for our children to give meaning to these vows.*

# CHAPTER FORTY

# Degrees of subservience

*Life was good to me, as long as I decided to give up what I
want,
As a child, I would listen to what my parents wanted and
desired,
Then when I grew up, I had a few friends who only desired
to be heard,
And then at work sometimes the only way to survive was
to be subservient,
As I got used to this life of subservience, I forgot about
myself,
Then I got married and the man in my life was all about
himself,
There was no day when I could willingly do what I liked to
do,
Every time I suppressed those desires of mine hoping to
make it work,
There were varying degrees of subservience in different
relationships in life,
I may not have known but when I loved myself less than
others' desires,*

*These were my choices choking my desires, that's when
freedom made its mark,
After years of struggle, I did what I desired and freed
myself from leading a subservient life.*

# CHAPTER FORTY-ONE

# Painkillers of life

*Sometimes in life, all you want is the pain to be benign,*
*But I had no painkillers in life,*
*For days together I could not face my life,*
*Nothing made sense to me,*
*Sometimes All I missed was to be heard at times like these,*
*As time went by I was lonely and scared,*
*Then one day I met a long-lost friend of mine,*
*And we talked about this life and that,*
*And I asked him for a few truths about life,*
*Asked him to tell me what he liked about me,*
*Ask him he if loved me for who I was and hugged him,*
*For all he did was heard me and went,*
*This was the painkiller that I needed in my life.*